D'Nealian® Handwriting
Practice and Review Workbook

Letter Instruction

Letter Practice

Everyday Writing

3

Copyright © by Savvas Learning Company LLC. All Rights Reserved. Printed in the United States of America.

This publication is protected by copyright, and permission should be obtained from the publisher prior to any prohibited reproduction, storage in a retrieval system, or transmission in any form or by any means, electronic, mechanical, photocopying, recording, or otherwise. The publisher hereby grants permission to reproduce pages, in part or in whole, for classroom use only, the number not to exceed the number of students in each class. Notice of copyright must appear on all copies. For information regarding permissions, request forms, and the appropriate contacts within the Savvas Learning Company Rights Management group, please send your query to the address below.

Savvas Learning Company LLC, 15 East Midland Avenue, Paramus, NJ 07652

Savvas™ and **Savvas Learning Company™** are the exclusive trademarks of Savvas Learning Company LLC in the U.S. and other countries.

Savvas Learning Company publishes through its famous imprints **Prentice Hall®** and **Scott Foresman®** which are exclusive registered trademarks owned by Savvas Learning Company LLC in the U.S. and/or other countries.

Savvas Realize™ is the exclusive trademark of Savvas Learning Company LLC in the U.S. and/or other countries.

D'Nealian® Handwriting is a registered trademark of Donald N. Thurber.

Unless otherwise indicated herein, any third party trademarks that may appear in this work are the property of their respective owners, and any references to third party trademarks, logos, or other trade dress are for demonstrative or descriptive purposes only. Such references are not intended to imply any sponsorship, endorsement, authorization, or promotion of Savvas Learning Company products by the owners of such marks, or any relationship between the owner and Savvas Learning Company LLC or its authors, licensees, or distributors.

ISBN-13: 978-0-673-57639-2
ISBN-10:   0-673-57639-6

Contents

Getting Started
Writing Posture 4
Writing in Cursive 5
Workbook Features 6
Evaluating Handwriting 7

Manuscript Letter Descriptions 8–9
Number Descriptions 9
Cursive Letter Descriptions 10–11

Manuscript Letter Review
Legibility: Letter Size and Form 12
Legibility: Letter Slant 13
Legibility: Letter and Word
   Spacing 14
Writing and Practicing
   aA, dD, oO, and gG 15–16
Writing and Practicing
   cC, eE, and sS 17–18
Writing and Practicing
   fF, bB, and lL 19–20
Writing and Practicing
   tT, hH, and kK 21–22
Writing and Practicing
   iI, uU, wW, and yY 23–24
Writing and Practicing
   jJ, rR, nN, mM, and pP 25–26
Writing and Practicing
   qQ, vV, zZ, and xX 27–28
Review and Evaluation 29–30

Writing Cursive Letters
Ready for Cursive 31
Strokes that Make Cursive
   Letters 32–34
Legibility: Letter Size and Form 35
Legibility: Letter Slant and
   Word Spacing 36
Writing and Practicing
   l, h, k, and t 37–38
Writing and Practicing
   i, u, and e 39–40
Writing and Practicing j and p 41–42
Review and Evaluation 43–44

Writing and Practicing
   a, d, and c 45–46
Writing and Practicing
   n, m, and x 47–48

Writing and Practicing
   g, y, and q 49–50
Review and Evaluation 51–52

Writing and Practicing
   o, w, and b 53–54
Writing and Practicing
   v and z 55–56
Writing and Practicing
   s and r 57–58
Writing and Practicing f 59–60
Review and Evaluation 61–62

Legibility: Letter Size and Form 63
Legibility: Letter Slant 64
Writing and Practicing
   A and C 65–66
Writing and Practicing
   E and O 67–68
Legibility: Letter and Word
   Spacing 69
Legibility: Sentence Spacing 70
Review and Evaluation 71–72

Writing and Practicing
   H and K 73–74
Writing and Practicing
   N, M, and U 75–76
Writing and Practicing
   V, W, and Y 77–78
Review and Evaluation 79–80

Writing and Practicing
   T and F 81–82
Writing and Practicing
   B, P, and R 83–84
Review and Evaluation 85–86

Writing and Practicing
   G, S, and I 87–88
Writing and Practicing
   Q, Z, and D 89–90
Writing and Practicing
   J, X, and L 91–92
Review and Evaluation 93–94

Index 95

Name _____

Get ready to write.
Use good posture. Sit up tall.
Put your feet on the floor.
Hold your pencil lightly.

Slant your paper.

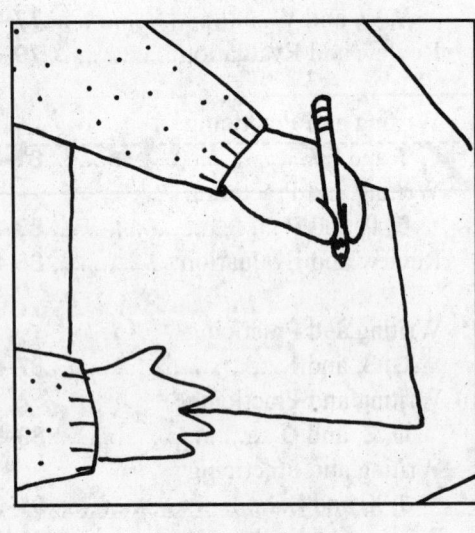

left-handed

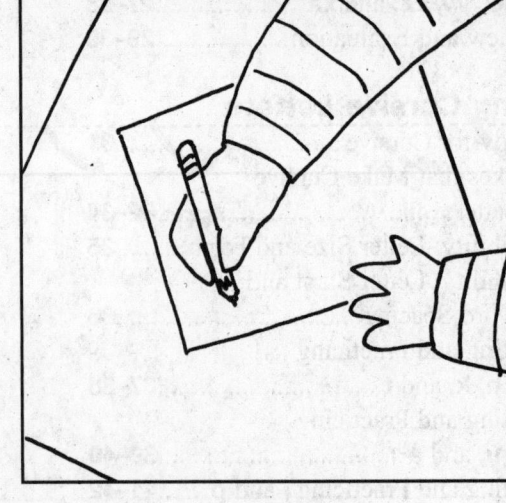

right-handed

Children model posture, pencil grip, arm position, and paper position for writing.

Contents

Getting Started
Writing Posture 4
Writing in Cursive 5
Workbook Features 6
Evaluating Handwriting 7

Manuscript Letter Descriptions 8–9

Number Descriptions 9

Cursive Letter Descriptions 10–11

Manuscript Letter Review
Legibility: Letter Size and Form 12
Legibility: Letter Slant 13
Legibility: Letter and Word
 Spacing 14
Writing and Practicing
 aA, dD, oO, and gG 15–16
Writing and Practicing
 cC, eE, and sS 17–18
Writing and Practicing
 fF, bB, and lL 19–20
Writing and Practicing
 tT, hH, and kK 21–22
Writing and Practicing
 iI, uU, wW, and yY 23–24
Writing and Practicing
 jJ, rR, nN, mM, and pP 25–26
Writing and Practicing
 qQ, vV, zZ, and xX 27–28
Review and Evaluation 29–30

Writing Cursive Letters
Ready for Cursive 31
Strokes that Make Cursive
 Letters 32–34
Legibility: Letter Size and Form 35
Legibility: Letter Slant and
 Word Spacing 36
Writing and Practicing
 l, h, k, and t 37–38
Writing and Practicing
 i, u, and e 39–40
Writing and Practicing j and p 41–42
Review and Evaluation 43–44

Writing and Practicing
 a, d, and c 45–46
Writing and Practicing
 n, m, and x 47–48

Writing and Practicing
 g, y, and q 49–50
Review and Evaluation 51–52

Writing and Practicing
 o, w, and b 53–54
Writing and Practicing
 v and z 55–56
Writing and Practicing
 s and r 57–58
Writing and Practicing f 59–60
Review and Evaluation 61–62

Legibility: Letter Size and Form 63
Legibility: Letter Slant 64
Writing and Practicing
 A and C 65–66
Writing and Practicing
 E and O 67–68
Legibility: Letter and Word
 Spacing 69
Legibility: Sentence Spacing 70
Review and Evaluation 71–72

Writing and Practicing
 H and K 73–74
Writing and Practicing
 N, M, and U 75–76
Writing and Practicing
 V, W, and Y 77–78
Review and Evaluation 79–80

Writing and Practicing
 T and F 81–82
Writing and Practicing
 B, P, and R 83–84
Review and Evaluation 85–86

Writing and Practicing
 G, S, and I 87–88
Writing and Practicing
 Q, Z, and D 89–90
Writing and Practicing
 J, X, and L 91–92
Review and Evaluation 93–94

Index 95

Name _____

Get ready to write.
Use good posture. Sit up tall.
Put your feet on the floor.
Hold your pencil lightly.

Slant your paper.

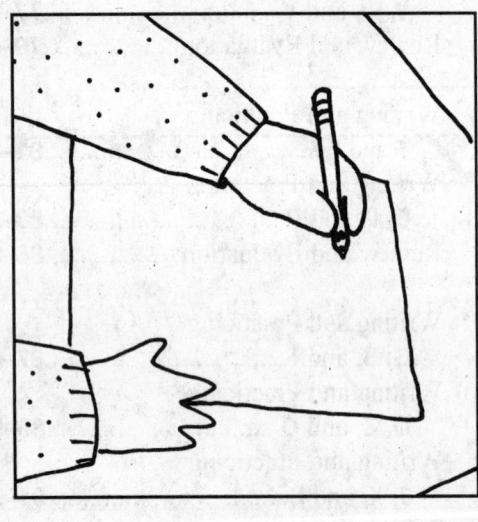

left-handed

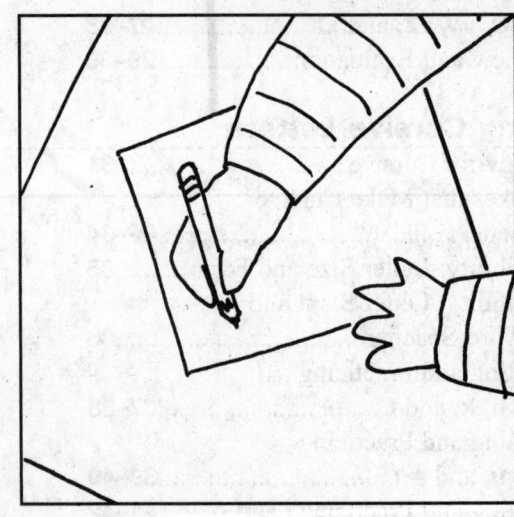

right-handed

Children model posture, pencil grip, arm position, and paper position for writing.

Name _____

Writing in Cursive

Look at the difference between manuscript writing and cursive writing.

hands
Manuscript letters are not joined together.

hands
Cursive letters are connected.

Cursive letters are connected.

These are connecting strokes. Trace them.

| uphill | short uphill | overhill | sidestroke |

Some cursive letters have new letter forms. Trace the letters.

f r s v z

Children learn the difference between manuscript writing and cursive writing.

5

Name _____

Use the Workbook Features

The dot shows you where to begin a letter.
The arrow shows you how to make the stroke.
The lines are for tracing letters. Tracing helps you learn how to form letters.

Use Lines to Learn Letter Size

top line
middle line
baseline (topline)
middle line (descender line)

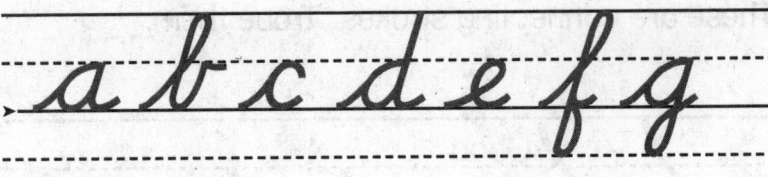

Where do you write small letters, tall letters, and letters that fall?
Trace the small letters in blue.
Trace the tall letters in green.
Trace letters that fall in red.
Circle the letter that you traced twice.

Name _____

Evaluate Your Handwriting

Check your letters for size, shape, slant, and spacing.

Size Are my letters written between the correct lines?

Shape Are curved lines curved? Are straight lines straight? Are closed letters closed?

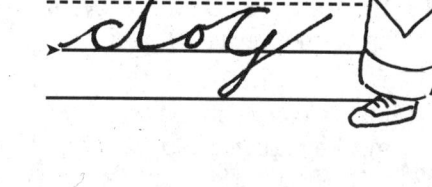

Slant Do all my letters slant the same way?

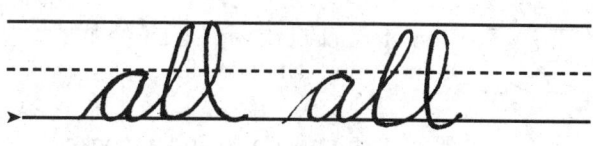

Spacing Are my letters too close or too far apart? Are my words too close or too far apart?

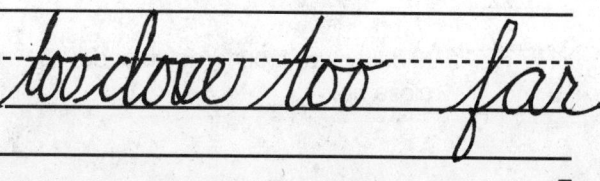

Children learn how to evaluate their handwriting.

Manuscript Letter Descriptions

Lower-case Letters

a — Middle start; around down, close up, down, and a monkey tail.

b — Top start; slant down, around, up, and a tummy.

c — Start below the middle; curve up, around, down, up, and stop.

d — Middle start; around down, touch, up high, down, and a monkey tail.

e — Start between the middle and bottom; curve up, around, touch, down, up, and stop.

f — Start below the top; curve up, around, and slant down. Cross.

g — Middle start; around down, close up, down under water, and a fishhook.

h — Top start; slant down, up over the hill, and a monkey tail.

i — Middle start; slant down and a monkey tail. Add a dot.

j — Middle start; slant down under water and a fishhook. Add a dot.

k — Top start; slant down, up into a little tummy, and a monkey tail.

l — Top start; slant down and a monkey tail.

m — Middle start; slant down, up over the hill, up over the hill again, and a monkey tail.

n — Middle start; slant down, up over the hill, and a monkey tail.

o — Middle start; around down and close up.

p — Middle start; slant down under water, up, around, and a tummy.

q — Middle start; around down, close up, down under water, and a backward fishhook.

r — Middle start; slant down, up, and a roof.

s — Start below the middle; curve up, around, down, and a snake tail.

t — Top start; slant down and a monkey tail. Cross.

u — Middle start; down, around, up, down, and a monkey tail.

v — Middle start; slant down right and slant up right.

w — Middle start; down, around, up, and down, around, up again.

x — Middle start; slant down right, and a monkey tail. Cross down left.

y — Middle start; down, around, up, down under water, and a fishhook.

z — Middle start; over right, slant down left, and over right.

Capital Letters

A — Top start; slant down left. Same start; slant down right. Middle bar across.

B — Top start; slant down, up, around halfway, close, around again, and close.

C — Start below the top; curve up, around, down, up, and stop.

D — Top start; slant down, up, around, and close.

8

E — Top start; over left, slant down, and over right. Middle bar across.

F — Top start; over left and slant down. Middle bar across.

G — Start below the top, curve up, around, down, up, and over left.

H — Top start; slant down. Another top start, to the right; slant down. Middle bar across.

I — Top start; slant down. Cross the top and the bottom line.

J — Top start; slant down and curve up left.

K — Top start; slant down. Another top start, to the right; slant down left, touch, slant down right, and a monkey tail.

L — Top start; slant down and over right.

M — Top start; slant down. Same start; slant down right halfway, slant up right, and slant down.

N — Top start; slant down. Same start; slant down right, and slant up.

O — Top start; around down and close up.

P — Top start; slant down, up, around halfway, and close.

Q — Top start; around down and close up. Cross with a curve down right.

R — Top start; slant down, up, around halfway, close, slant down right, and a monkey tail.

S — Start below the top; curve up, around, down, and a snake tail.

T — Top start; slant down. Cross the line at the top.

U — Top start; slant down, around, up, down, and a monkey tail.

V — Top start; slant down right and slant up right.

W — Top start; slant down right, slant up right, slant down right, and slant up right again.

X — Top start; slant down right and a monkey tail. Cross down left.

Y — Top start; slant down right halfway. Another top start, to the right; slant down left, and touch on the way.

Z — Top start; over right, slant down left, and over right.

Number Descriptions

1 — Top start; slant down.

2 — Start below the top; curve up, around, and slant down left, and over right.

3 — Start below the top; curve up, around halfway; around again, up, and stop.

4 — Top start; down halfway; over right. Another top start, to the right; slant down and through.

5 — Top start; over left; slant down halfway; curve around, down, up, and stop.

6 — Top start; slant down, and curve around; up, and close.

7 — Top start; over right; slant down left.

8 — Start below the top; curve up, around, down; a snake tail; slant up right; through, and touch.

9 — Top start; curve down, around, close; slant down.

10 — Top start; slant down. Another top start to the right; curve down, around, and close.

9

Cursive Letter Descriptions

Lower-case Letters

a — Overhill; back, around down, close up, down, and up.

b — Uphill high; loop down, around, up, and sidestroke.

c — Overhill; back, around, down, and up.

d — Overhill; back, around down, touch, up high, down, and up.

e — Uphill; loop down, through, and up.

f — Uphill high; loop down under water, loop up right, touch, and up.

g — Overhill; back, around down, close up, down under water, loop up left, and through.

h — Uphill high; loop down, up over the hill, and up.

i — Uphill; down, and up. Add a dot.

j — Uphill; down under water, loop up left, and through. Add a dot.

k — Uphill high; loop down, up into a little tummy, slant down right, and up.

l — Uphill high; loop down, and up.

m — Overhill; down, up over the hill, up over the hill again, and up.

n — Overhill; down, up over the hill, and up.

o — Overhill; back, around down, close up, and sidestroke.

p — Uphill; down under water, up, around into a tummy, and up.

q — Overhill; back, around down, close up, down under water, loop up right, touch, and up.

r — Uphill; sidestroke, down, and up.

s — Uphill; down, around, close, and up.

t — Uphill high; down, and up. Cross.

u — Uphill; down, around, up, down, and up.

v — Overhill; down, around, up, and sidestroke.

w — Uphill; down, around, up, down, around, up again, and sidestroke.

x — Overhill; slant down right, and up. Cross down left.

y — Overhill; down, around, up, down under water, loop up left, and through.

z — Overhill; around down, around again, and down under water, loop up left, and through.

Capital Letters

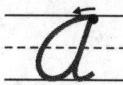 Top start; around down, close up, down, and up.

 Top start; down, up, around halfway, around again, touch, sidestroke, and stop.

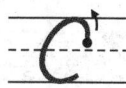 Start below the top; curve up, around, down, and up.

 Top start; down, loop right, curve up, around, close, loop right, through, and stop.

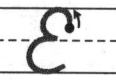 Start below the top; curve up, around to the middle, around again to the bottom line, and up.

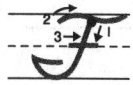 Start below the top; down, around, up, and sidestroke. Wavy cross and a straight cross.

 Bottom start; uphill high, loop through the middle, up, curve down, around, through the uphill, sidestroke, and stop.

 Start below the top; make a cane. Top start, to the right; down, up, left, touch, loop right, through, and stop.

 Start below the middle; sidestroke left, curve down, around, uphill high, loop down, and up.

 Bottom start; curve up, around, touch on the way down under water, loop up left, and through.

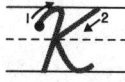 Start below the top; make a cane. Top start, to the right; slant down left, touch, slant down right, and up.

 Start below the top; uphill, loop down, loop right, and up.

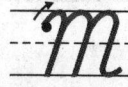 Start below the top; make a cane, up over the hill, up over the hill again, and up.

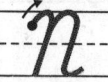 Start below the top; make a cane, up over the hill, and up.

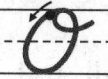 Top start; around down, close up, loop right, through, and stop.

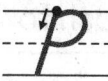 Top start; down, up, around halfway, and close.

 Start below the top; curve up, around, down, loop right, and up.

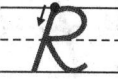 Top start; down, up, around halfway, close, slant down right, and up.

 Bottom start; uphill high, loop through the middle, curve down, around, through the uphill, sidestroke, and stop.

 Start below the top; down, around, up, and sidestroke. Wavy cross.

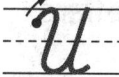 Start below the top; make a cane, around, up, down, and up.

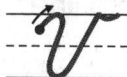 Start below the top; make a cane, around, slant up right, sidestroke, and stop.

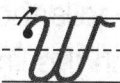 Start below the top; make a cane, around, up, down, around, up again, sidestroke, and stop.

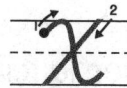 Start below the top; curve up, slant down right, and up. Cross down left.

 Start below the top; make a cane, around up, down under water, loop up left, and through.

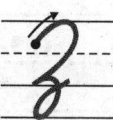 Start below the top; curve up, around, down, around again, and down under water, loop up left, and through.

Name _____

Letter Size and Form

Manuscript letters can be **small, tall,** or have **descenders.** Can you name each row of letters?

a c e i m n o r s u v w x z

b d f h k l t

g j p q y

Small letters sit on the bottom line. They touch the middle line. Write three small letters.

Tall letters also sit on the bottom line. They touch the top line. Write three tall letters.

Letters with **descenders** have tails that go down under the bottom line and touch the line below. Write three letters with descenders.

Handwriting is easy to read when letters are formed correctly. Letters like **b, d, o,** and **g** must be closed. The letters **t** and **f** must be crossed. The letters **i** and **j** are dotted.

Can you read the phrase below?

big dog

The phrase is **big dog.** Why is it so hard to read?

Write the phrase **big dog** correctly.

Name _____

Letter Slant

Slant all your letters the same way. Find the slant that is right for you. Then keep that slant.

Some writers slant their letters to the right.

Some writers slant their letters to the left.

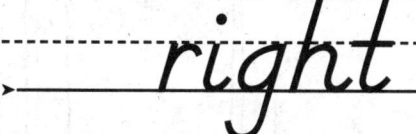 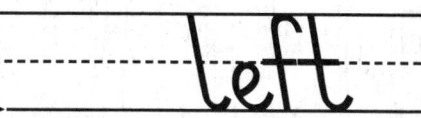

Some writers make their letters straight up and down.

Do not slant your letters different ways.

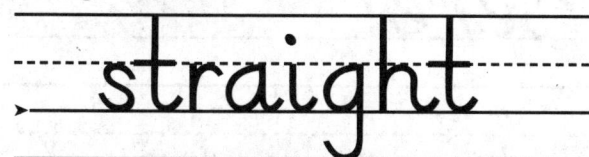

Choose a slant. Write: Monkeys are spunky!

_____
_____
▸ _____

13

Name _____

Letter and Word Spacing

Spacing is important. Think about building a fence.
If the boards are too close together, it looks messy.
If the boards are too far apart, what might happen?

When you write, spacing is important too. Letters, words, and punctuation marks should not be too close together or too far apart. Write these sentences. Use a finger space between words.

Letme outo fhere!

Idon't lik e fences.

Name

Writing Manuscript aA, dD, oO, and gG

Write the lower-case letters.

a					a

d					d

o					o

g					g

Write the capital letters.

A					D

O					G

Write the book title.
A Grand Old Dog

Name _____

Practicing Manuscript aA, dD, oO, and gG

If dogs had their own circus, you might see these acts.
Write the names of the acts.

Aerial Airedales   **Diving Dachshund**

The circus also would need workers. Write the names of the working dogs.

Old English sheepdog

German shepherd

Name _____

Writing Manuscript cC, eE, and sS

Write the lower-case letters.

c   c

e   e

s   s

Write the capital letters.

C   E   S

Write the names.
English cocker spaniel

_____

Shetland sheepdog

_____

Name _____

Practicing Manuscript cC, eE, and sS

Make up one or two titles for each book. Write them.
Use some words from the box.

The	of	the	in	Cocker Spaniel
Case	Sleeping	a	Eye	Sheepdog
Sings	School	Open	A	Opera

Name _____

Writing Manuscript fF, bB, and lL

Write the lower-case letters.

f _____ f

b _____ b

l _____ l

Write the capital letters.

F   B   L

Write the names.

Libby
_____

Fluffy
_____

Fido's Biscuits
_____

Name _____

Practicing Manuscript fF, bB, and lL

Billy must get his dog, Fair Lady, ready for a dog show. Look at the list. Write three things you think are most important for Billy to do.

To Do List

Bathe and brush Fair Lady.
Wash Fair Lady's pillow.
Give Fair Lady treats.
Walk Fair Lady in a circle.
Teach Fair Lady to "heel."

1. _____

2. _____

3. _____

Name _____

Writing Manuscript tT, hH, and kK

Write the lower-case letters.

t   t

h   h

k   k

Write the capital letters.

T   H   K

Write the name and the sentence.
Heidi

Take Heidi to the Happy Trails Kennel.

21

Name _____

Practicing Manuscript tT, hH, and kK

Thad's dog, Holly, has been missing for several days. Help him find her by filling in the missing words. Use words from the box.

key	Holly	terrier
Kenmore	Thad	honey

LOST

My dog _____ is missing. She was last seen

on _____ Street. She is a _____

the color of _____ . The tag around her neck

looks like a _____ . Please call _____

at (555) 312-1222.

Name _____

Writing Manuscript iI, uU, wW, and yY

Write the lower-case letters.

i   i

u   u

w   w

y   y

Write the capital letters.

I   U

W   Y

Write the sentence.
Uncle Yoshio and I saw a cute puppy.

Name _____

Practicing Manuscript iI, uU, wW, and yY

Read Juan's letter. Write words from the box to complete the sentences.

Uncle Will	summer
walking	I
Yorkshire terriers	Siberian huskies

May 31, 1997

Dear Alicia,
  Guess what! (1) have a (2) job! (3) helped me get it. I am (4) dogs for people. My favorite breeds are (5) and (6). Please write back soon.

Your cousin,
Juan

1.
2.
3.
4.
5.
6.

Name _____

Writing Manuscript jJ, rR, nN, mM, and pP

Write the lower-case letters.

j   j
r   r
n   n
m   m
p   p

Write the capital letters.

J   R   N
M   P

Write the sentence.
Poodles run and jump.

25

Name _____

Practicing Manuscript jJ, rR, nN, mM, and pP

Match the names and actions according to first letters. Then write sentences that tell what the people and dogs are doing. The first one is done for you.

Names		Actions	
Paul	Marj	jumping	running
Nate	Roxy	napping	mailing
	Jake		pitching

1. *Paul is pitching a ball.*

2. _____

3. _____

4. _____

5. _____

Name _____

Writing Manuscript qQ, vV, zZ, and xX

Write the lower-case letters.

q   q

v   v

z   z

x   x

Write the capital letters.

Q   V   Z   X

Write the sentence.
Liz and Xavier Quinn pose with Vic and Zeus.

Name _____

Practicing Manuscript qQ, vV, zZ, and xX

Pretend you live in this small town. Answer the questions by writing names of places in the town.

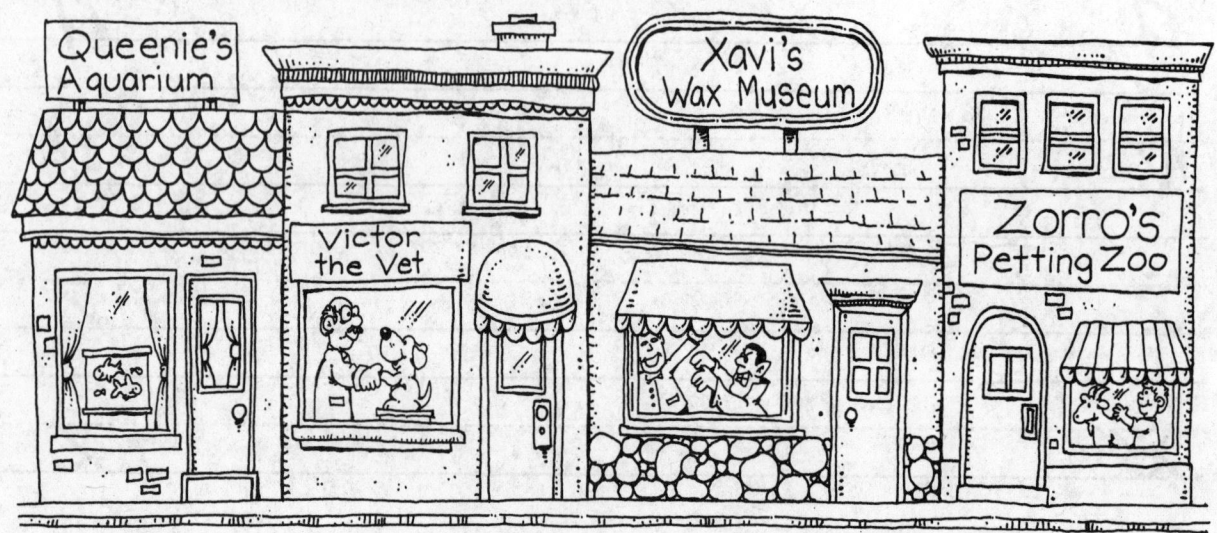

1. Where do you take your dog when he is sick?

2. Where can you find statues that look like real people?

3. If you wanted to buy a goldfish for your brother, where would you go?

4. What would be a good place for a birthday party?

28

Name _____

Review

The children want to give their dog a bath. Use the words in the box. Write a name under each picture. Then write a list of things the children might use to bathe their pup.

water	Jeff	fork	Blackie	brush	hose
Annie	towel	hat	soap	tub	car

_____ _____ _____

Things We Need to Wash Our Dog

_____ _____

_____ _____

_____ _____

_____ _____

Name _____

Evaluation

Write the words and sentences.

Dog Washing Today – $1.00

Jeff will do the shampooing.

Annie will dry each dog.

✓ **Check Your Handwriting**   Yes   No

Are your tall letters tall, your small letters small, and your letters with descenders touching the line below? ☐ ☐

Do all your letters slant the same way? ☐ ☐

Remember: Letters come in three sizes—tall, small, and with descenders. Also, your letters should all slant the same way.

Name _____

Get Ready for Cursive!

In **manuscript writing**, letters are not joined together.

Cubs win 11-7!

In **cursive writing**, most letters are joined together.

Cubs win 11-7!

Follow these directions:
1. Read the words in cursive.
2. Make a ‿ under places where the letters are joined.
3. Then write the words in manuscript. The first one is done for you.

game   game

team

score

Name _____

Strokes That Make Cursive Letters: Uphill Strokes

uphill strokes

To write cursive **l, h, k, t, i, u,** and **e**, you add an **uphill stroke** to each letter you already know. These letters already have an ending stroke. Now look at **j** and **p**. To write them, begin with an uphill stroke and add an ending stroke.

With your finger, trace the uphill stroke in each letter. Circle the ending stroke in each letter.

l h k t i u e j p

An uphill stroke can be tall or short. Practice each one.

Now look at the letters below. Notice that they begin with uphill strokes. Trace the words.

like   like
jeep   jeep
hut   hut

32

Name _____

Strokes That Make Cursive Letters: Overhill Strokes

overhill stroke

To write cursive **a, d, c, n, m, x, g, y,** and **q,** you add an **overhill stroke** to each letter you already know. With your finger, trace the overhill stroke in each letter. The letters **g, y,** and **q** also need ending strokes added to them. Notice how the ending stroke is formed in each letter.

a d c n m x g y q

Practice the overhill stroke.

Look at the letters below. They begin with overhill strokes. Circle where the letters begin and end. Trace the word.

m a d   mad

Which letters below have uphill strokes? Which letters have overhill strokes? Trace the word.

p a n   pan

Name _____

Strokes That Make Cursive Letters: Sidestrokes

sidestroke

The letters **o, w,** and **b** end with a **sidestroke.** With your finger trace the sidestroke in each letter. Which letter begins with an overhill stroke? Which letters begin with uphill strokes?

o w b

Practice the sidestroke.

Look at the letters below. Notice where they begin and end. A sidestroke letter always joins the following letter near the middle line. This changes the beginning stroke of the following letter. Notice how the sidestroke changes **n, e,** and **a** in **on, wet,** and **bat.** Trace the words.

on wet bat
on wet bat

Cursive letters **v, z, s, r,** and **f** look different from the letters you already know. Which letter ends with a sidestroke? Which two letters begin with overhill strokes? Which three letters begin with uphill strokes? Trace the letters.

v z s r f

34

Name _____

Letter Size and Form

a c e i m n o r s u v w x
b d f h k l t
f g j p q y z

Cursive letters come in the same three sizes as manuscript letters. There are small letters, tall letters, and letters with descenders. Which tall letter also has a descender?

To make your handwriting clear and easy to read, be sure to form your letters correctly.

Some cursive letters must be closed.

a o d

To practice closing letters, trace these letters.

a o d

Some cursive letters have loops.

b g f

To practice looping letters, trace these letters.

b g f

Some cursive letters need retracing. Go over a line that you've already written.

d p t

To practice retracing, trace these letters.

d p t

35

Name _____

Letter Slant and Word Spacing

When you write in cursive, slant all your letters the same way. You may slant your letters to the right or to the left. You may write them straight up and down. Do not slant your letters different ways. Choose the slant you like best. Trace the word.

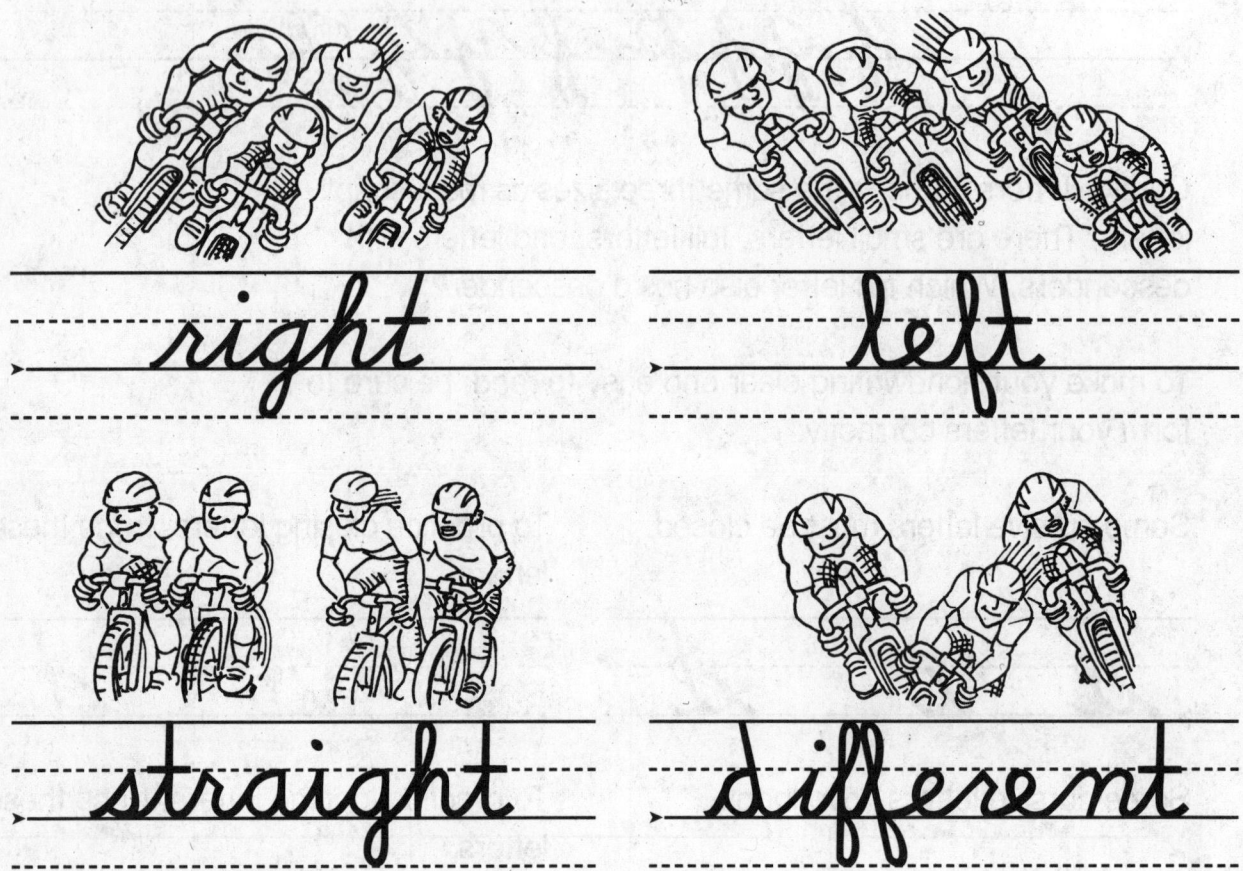

Which writing is hard to read? Why is it hard?

Use correct spacing when you write. The letters in a word should be evenly spaced. Leave more space between words than between letters in a word.

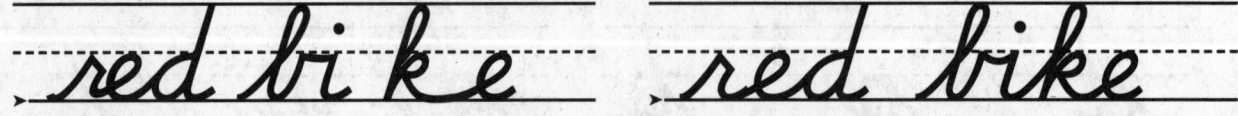

Which writing is easier to read? Circle it. Why is it easier?

36

Name _____

Writing Cursive l, h, k, and t

Cursive letters **l**, **h**, **k**, and **t** look like their manuscript forms. Add an uphill stroke to write the cursive letter. Trace and write the letters.

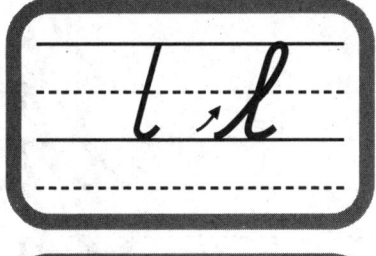 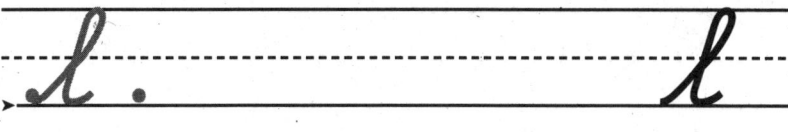

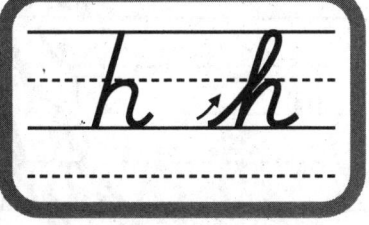 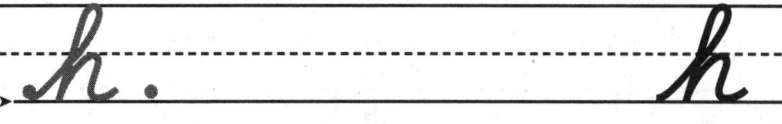

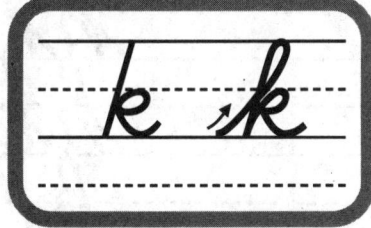 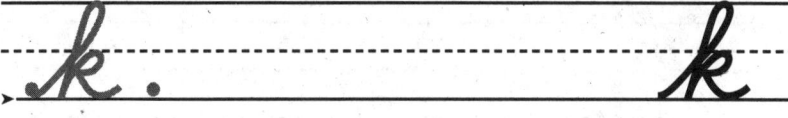

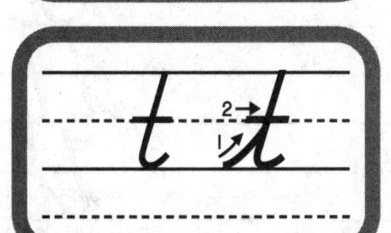 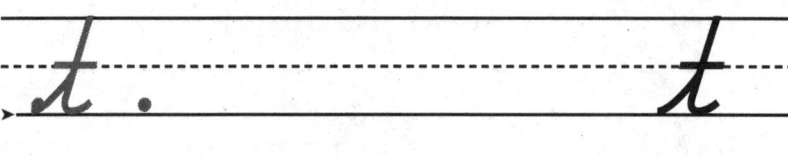

Amy is packing for a trip to Hawaii. Use cursive to write the first letter of each item she will take.

   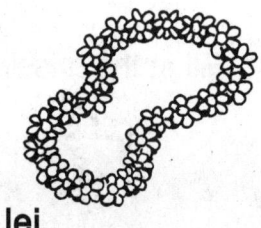

kite   toothbrush   hat   lei

Letter Descriptions: l: Uphill high; loop down, and up. **h:** Uphill high; loop down, up over the hill, and up.
k: Uphill high; loop down, up into a little tummy, slant down right, and up. **t:** Uphill high; down, and up. Cross.

Name

Practicing Cursive l, h, k, and t

When you write in cursive, you join the letters. Most letters join at the bottom line. Trace and write the joined letters.

ll ll

lh lh

lk lk

lt lt

hh hh

hl hl

ht ht

kl kl

tt tt

tl tl

th th

Fill in the missing letters. Join the letters at the bottom line.

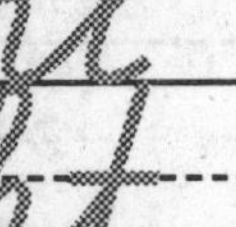

milk

mi

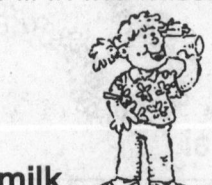

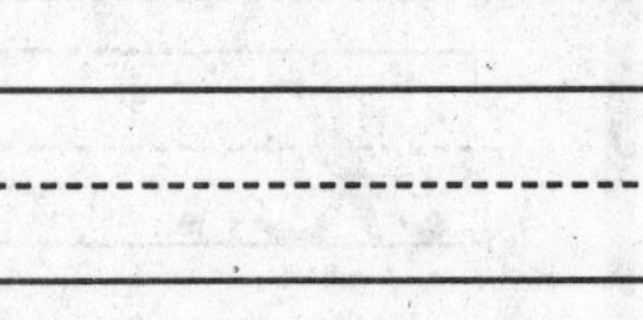

hill

hi

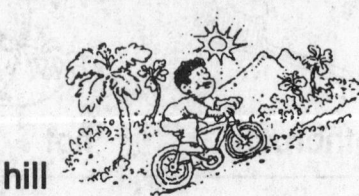

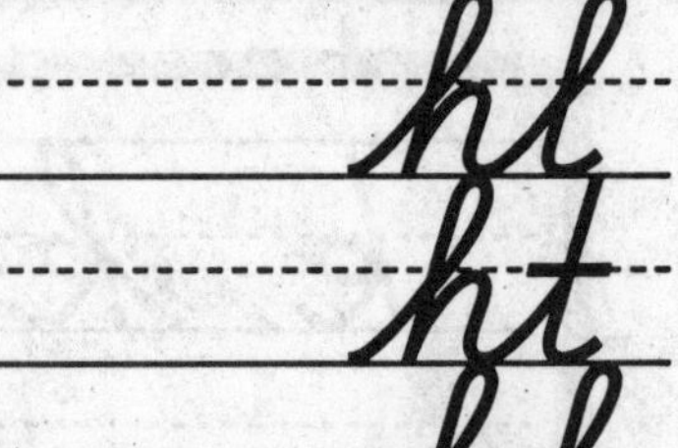

path

pa

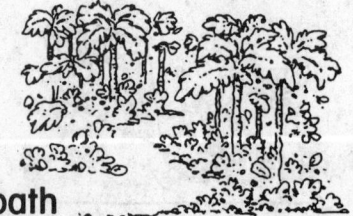

Name _____

Writing Cursive i, u, and e

Cursive letters **i**, **u**, and **e** look like their manuscript forms. Add an uphill stroke to write the cursive letter. Trace and write the letters.

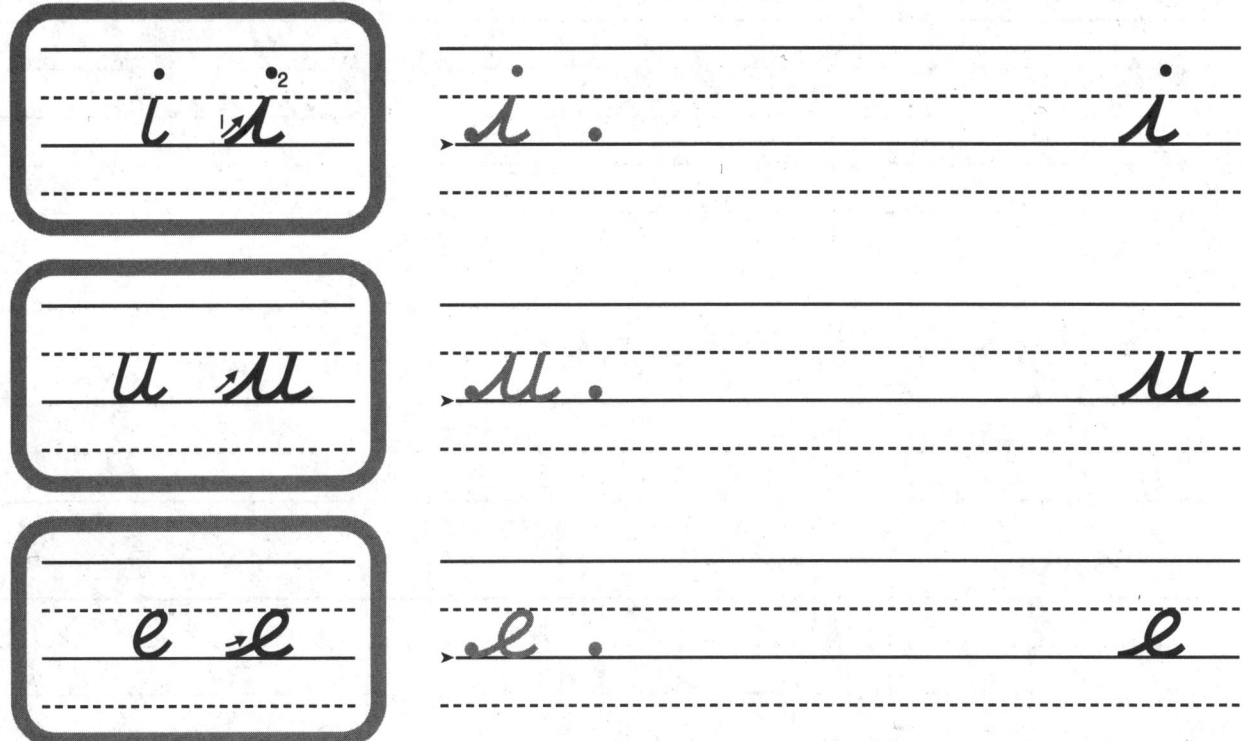

Trace and write the words.

kit

hull

let

jet

kite

tell

Letter Descriptions: i: Uphill; down, and up. Add a dot. **u:** Uphill; down, around, up, down, and up.
e: Uphill; loop down, through, and up.

39

Name _____

Practicing Cursive i, u, and e

Trace and write the words and phrases.

lei

lei

hut

hut

hill

hill

hit

hit

till

till

tie

tie

like the hike

like the hike

the little ukulele

the little ukulele

40

Name

Writing Cursive j and p

Cursive letters **j** and **p** look very much like their manuscript forms. To write them in cursive, you must add an uphill stroke and an ending stroke. Trace and write the letters.

Trace and write the words.

jet

pet

peek

up

help

keep

Letter Descriptions: j: Uphill; down under water, loop up left, and through. Add a dot. **p:** Uphill; down under water, up, around into a tummy, and up.

Name _____

Practicing Cursive j and p

Trace and write the words and phrases.

jeep

jeep

pit

pit

put

put

jut

jut

pull

pull

peel

peel

the little pet

the little pet

like the help

like the help

Name _____

Review

Tim has to follow directions to get to the island's treasure.
Use words from the box to complete the directions.

pull   tulip   hike   jeep   jet   hill

First, (1) open the steel door. Drive your (2) to the runway. Fly the (3) plane to the steep (4). Leave the plane and (5) to the (6) garden. Under the white tulip is a chest of gold coins.

1. _____
2. _____
3. _____
4. _____
5. _____
6. _____

Name _____

Evaluation

Write the words and phrases.

Remember: Cross the letter **t** and dot the letters **i** and **j**. Leave a finger space between words.

pull the jeep

like the jet

kept the ukulele

hike uphill

✓ **Check Your Handwriting**   Yes   No
   Did you close the letter **t**?   ☐   ☐
   Did you dot the letters **i** and **j**? ☐   ☐
   Did you leave enough space between words? ☐ ☐

Name _____

Writing Cursive a, d, and c

Cursive letters **a**, **d**, and **c** look like their manuscript forms. Add an overhill stroke to write the cursive letter. Trace and write the letters.

a a   *a .*   *a*

d d   *d .*   *d*

c c   *c .*   *c*

Trace and write the words.

dad   **child**   **cap**

dad   *child*   *cap*

head   **call**   **catch**

head   *call*   *catch*

Letter Descriptions a: Overhill; back, around down, close up, down, and up. **d:** Overhill; back, around down, touch, up high, down, and up. **c:** Overhill; back, around, down, and up.

Name _____

Practicing Cursive a, d, and c

Trace and write the phrases.

a dad and child

a dad and child

a puddle ahead

a puddle ahead

each tall athlete

each tall athlete

that lake path

that lake path

Name _____

Writing Cursive n, m, and x

Cursive letters **n**, **m**, and **x** look like their manuscript forms. Add an overhill stroke to write the cursive letter. Trace and write the letters.

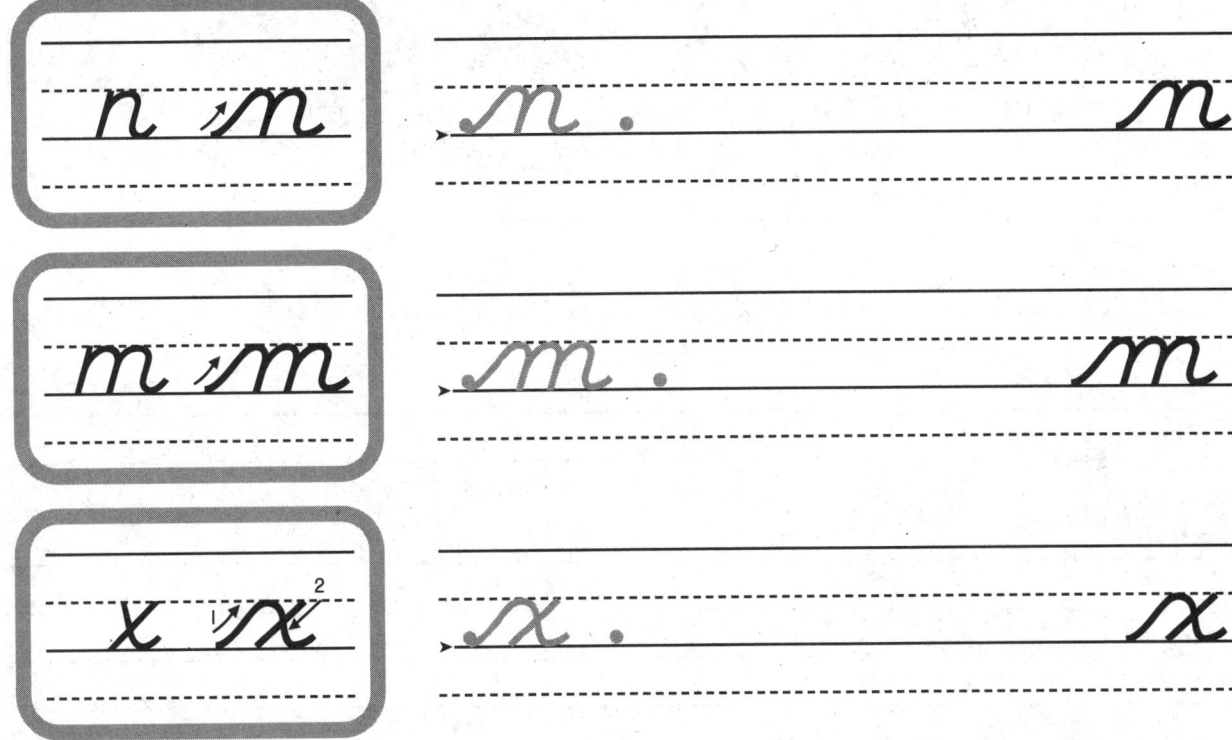

Trace and write the words.

lunch

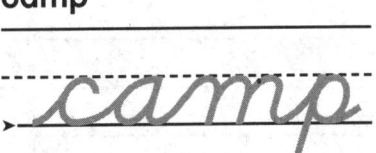

camp

camp

milk

milk

next exit

next exit

Letter Descriptions **n:** Overhill; down, up over the hill, and up. **m:** Overhill; down, up over the hill, up over the hill again, and up. **x:** Overhill; slant down right, and up. Cross down left.

47

Name _____

Practicing Cursive n, m, and x

Trace and write the phrases.

nice time to picnic

nice time to picnic

excellent limeade

excellent limeade

pink mint punch

pink mint punch

a damp napkin

a damp napkin

Name _____

Writing Cursive g, y, and q

Cursive letters **g, y,** and **q** look like their manuscript forms. To write them in cursive, you must add an overhill stroke and an ending stroke. Trace and write the letters.

Trace and write the words.

tiny　　　　　　　　quilt　　　　　　　　light

tiny　　　　　　　*quilt*　　　　　　　*light*

Letter Descriptions g: Overhill; back, around down, close up, down under water, loop up left, and through.
y: Overhill; down, around, up, down under water, loop up left, and through.   **q:** Overhill; back, around down, close up, down under water, loop up right, touch, and up.

Name _____

Practicing Cursive g, y, and q

Trace and write the phrases.

a jungle gym

a jungle gym

play equipment

play equipment

a quick game

a quick game

quietly laughing

quietly laughing

Name _____

Review

Ms. True's class is having a picnic. Some children will work on the menu and others will plan the fun. Decide where each word belongs and write it under the correct heading. Write leftover words at the bottom.

| jelly | dance | taxi | chicken | catch | tuna |
| game | cake | tag | hula | juice | quilt |

Food   **Fun**

Leftover Words

Name _____

Evaluation

Write the phrases.

Remember: Descenders should touch the line below. Also, space your writing so tall letters do not run into descenders.

a healthy meal

a healthy meal

next quiet picnic

next quiet picnic

hugging a child

hugging a child

my cuddly quilt

my cuddly quilt

✓ **Check Your Handwriting** Yes No
Do your descenders touch the line below? ☐ ☐
Do any of your tall letters run into descenders? ☐ ☐

Name _____

Review

Ms. True's class is having a picnic. Some children will work on the menu and others will plan the fun. Decide where each word belongs and write it under the correct heading. Write leftover words at the bottom.

| jelly | dance | taxi | chicken | catch | tuna |
| game | cake | tag | hula | juice | quilt |

Food

Fun

Leftover Words

Name _____

Evaluation

Write the phrases.

Remember: Descenders should touch the line below. Also, space your writing so tall letters do not run into descenders.

a healthy meal

a healthy meal

next quiet picnic

next quiet picnic

hugging a child

hugging a child

my cuddly quilt

my cuddly quilt

✓ **Check Your Handwriting**　　　　　　　　　Yes　No
　Do your descenders touch the line below?　☐　☐
　Do any of your tall letters run into descenders?　☐　☐

Name _____

Writing Cursive o, w, and b

Cursive **o, w,** and **b** look much like their manuscript forms. Begin cursive **o** with an overhill stroke. Begin cursive **w** and **b** with an uphill stroke. Each letter ends with a sidestroke near the middle line. Trace and write the letters.

Remember that **o, w,** and **b** join the next letter near the middle line. This changes the beginning stroke of the next letter. Trace and write the joined letters and words.

ow ow
bo bo

bow   wood   block

Letter Descriptions o: Overhill; back, around down, close up, and sidestroke. **w:** Uphill; down, around, up, down, around, up again, and sidestroke. **b:** Uphill high; loop down, around, up, and sidestroke.

Name _____

Practicing Cursive o, w, and b

School bands are fun. Trace and write the phrases.

girl with piccolo

girl with piccolo

one white banjo

one white banjo

low blue piano

low blue piano

Name _____

Writing Cursive v and z

Cursive **v** and **z** do not look like manuscript **v** and **z**. Notice that cursive **v** ends with a sidestroke. Trace and write the letters.

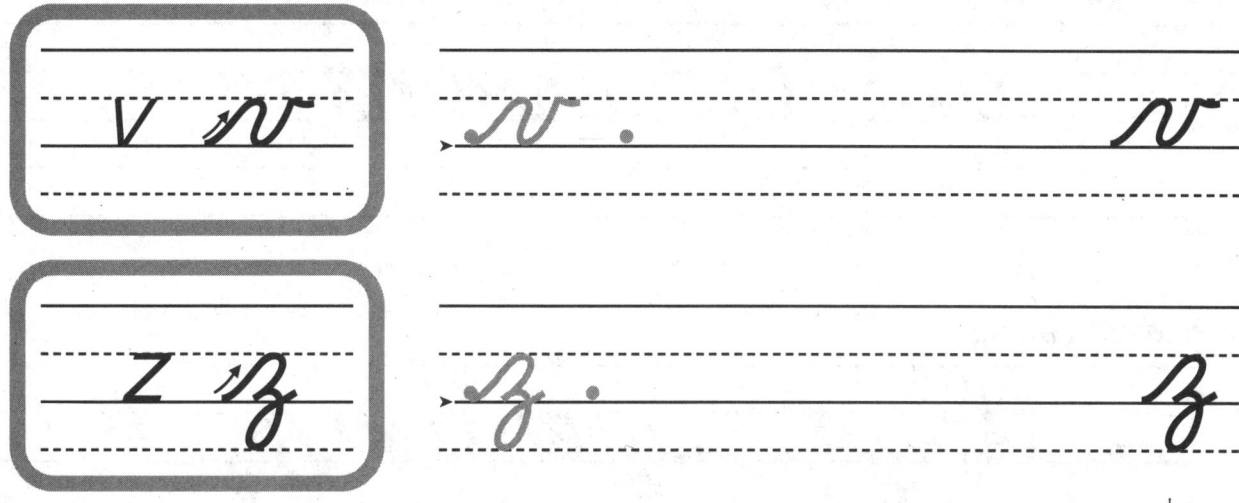

Remember that **v** joins the next letter near the middle line. Trace and write the words.

violin

violin

velvet

velvet

buzz

buzz

cozy

cozy

hazy

hazy

Letter Descriptions **v**: Overhill; down, around, up, and sidestroke. **z**: Overhill; around down, around again, and down under water, loop up left, and through.

Name _____

Practicing Cursive v and z

Trace and write the phrases.

a lovely event

a lovely event

a lazy evening

a lazy evening

very lively jazz

very lively jazz

Name _____

Writing Cursive s and r

Cursive **s** and **r** do not look like manuscript **s** and **r**.
Trace and write the letters.

 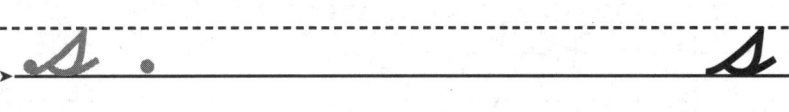

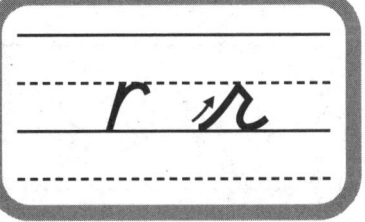 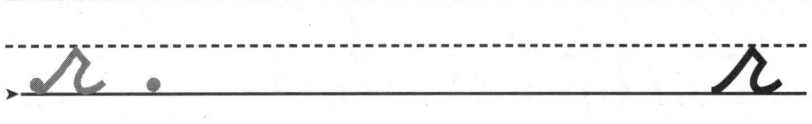

Trace and write the words.

strings

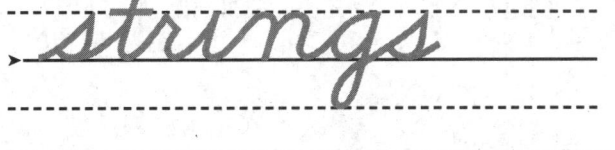

sing

songs

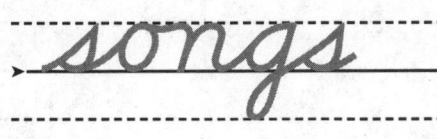

rhythm

Letter Descriptions s: Uphill; down, around, close, and up. **r:** Uphill; sidestroke, down, and up.

Name _____

Practicing Cursive s and r

Trace and write the phrases.

rock 'n' roll

rock 'n' roll

the school orchestra

the school orchestra

six percussion instruments

six percussion instruments

58

Name _____

Writing Cursive f

Cursive **f** does not look like its manuscript form.
Trace and write the letter.

 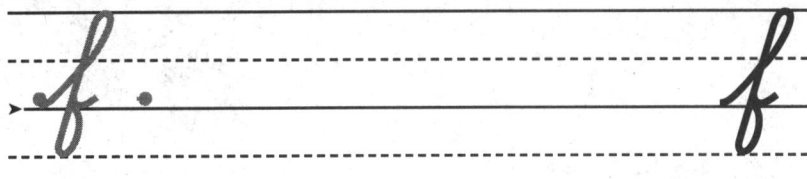

Trace and write the phrases.

fun

fast

first

treble clef

bass clef

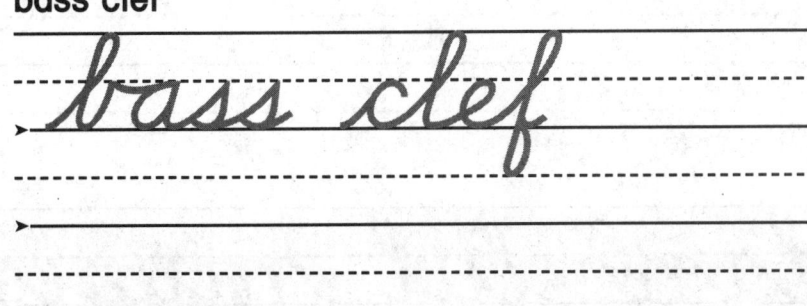

Letter Description **f:** Uphill high; loop down under water, loop up right, touch, and up.

59

Name _____

Practicing Cursive f

Trace and write the phrases.

flutes in front

flutes in front

a different effect

a different effect

friendly faces

friendly faces

very fanciful music

very fanciful music

Name _____

Review

Ismail's family owns a music store. Write items from the box that they might sell in their store.

xylophones	bazaars	wooden flutes
scarves	violins	ovens
pianos	jazz records	banjos

61

Name _____

Evaluation

Write the phrases.

Remember: The letters **o**, **w**, and **b** join the next letter near the middle line. Also, be sure each of your letters is formed correctly.

beautiful orchestra

a dozen violins

a bronze award

a velvet ribbon

room's yellow glow

✓ **Check Your Handwriting**   Yes   No
Are the letters in your words joined correctly? ☐ ☐
Is each letter formed correctly? ☐ ☐

Name _____

Letter Size and Form

Capital cursive letters all touch the top and bottom lines. Some capital letters also have descenders that touch the line below. To make your handwriting clear and easy to read, be sure to form your letters correctly.

Some capital letters are closed.

A   P

Some capital letters have loops.

G   O

You must retrace when you write some capital letters. That means you go over a line you've written.

M   R

Some capital letters have descenders. The descenders should touch the line below.

Y   Z

Trace the capital letters below. Then circle four letters that must be closed. Underline five letters that have loops. Put a ✔ above two letters that have descenders. Put a box around four letters that have retracing.

A B C D E F G H

I J K L M N O P Q

R S T U V W X Y Z

Name _____

Letter Slant

Slant your capital letters in the same direction as your lower-case letters. You may slant your letters to the right or to the left. You may write them straight up and down.

Right   *Left*

Straight   *Different*

Which writing is hard to read? Why is it hard?

Numbers and punctuation marks should slant in the same direction as your letters. Look at this sentence written two ways. Circle four letters and a number that slant the wrong way in the first sentence. Then trace the correct sentence.

May I use the computer at 1:00?
May I use the computer at 1:00?

Write this phrase. Slant all your letters the same way.
the same slant

_____

_____

Do your letters all slant the same way?   Yes ☐   No ☐

64

Name _____

Writing Cursive A and C

Capital cursive **A** looks different from manuscript **A**. Cursive **C** looks like its manuscript form. Trace and write the letters.

Trace and write the proper nouns. Always join **A** and **C** to the letters that follow them. Be sure to begin each proper noun with a capital. Put a comma between the name of the city and the name of the state.

Aspen, Colorado

Aspen, Colorado

Alex

Alex

Carmen

Carmen

Letter Descriptions A: Top start; around down, close up, down, and up. **C:** Start below the top; curve up, around, down, and up.

65

Name _____

Practicing Cursive A and C

Trace and write the sentences.
Anne's class visited Ace Computers.

Anne's class visited Ace Computers.

A guide named Cass gave them a tour.

A guide named Cass gave them a tour.

Ava and Curt know all about computers.

Ava and Curt know all about computers.

Name _____

Writing Cursive E and O

Cursive **E** looks a little like manuscript **E**. You can see manuscript **O** in cursive **O**. Trace and write the letters.

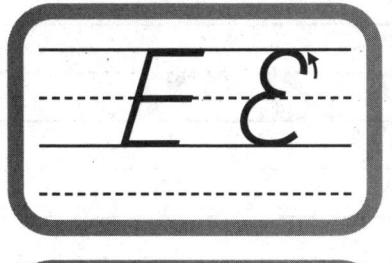 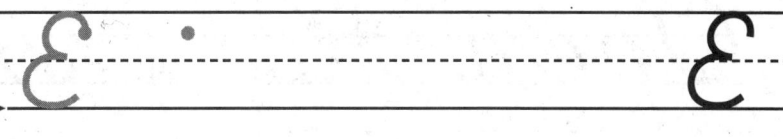

 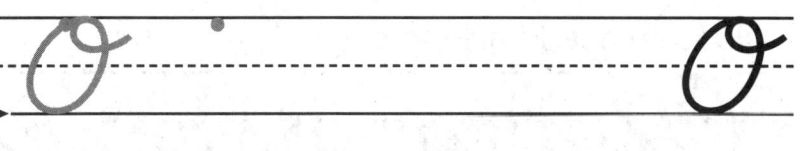

Trace and write the proper nouns. Always join **E** to the letter that follows it, but do not join **O**.

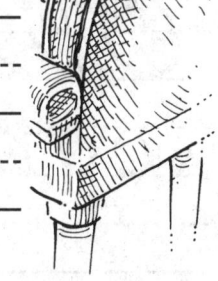

Elsa

Oliver

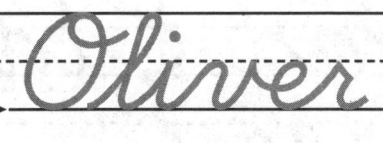

Eugene, Oregon

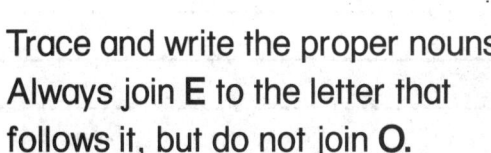

Letter Descriptions E: Start below the top; curve up, around to the middle, around again to the bottom line, and up. **O:** Top start; around down, close up, loop right, through, and stop.

67

Name _____

Practicing Cursive E and O

Trace and write the sentences.

Open the program.

Open the program.

Olivia pressed Enter to begin.

Olivia pressed Enter to begin.

Otis and Eddie share computer E.

Otis and Eddie share computer E.

Name _____

Letter and Word Spacing

Space letters and words evenly. Use more space between words than between letters in a word. Write the phrases. Answer each question.

school computer lab

school computer lab

a color monitor

a color monitor

Are your letters evenly spaced?   Yes ☐   No ☐

full-sized keyboard

full-sized keyboard

for word processing

for word processing

Do you use the correct word spacing?   Yes ☐   No ☐

Name _____

Sentence Spacing

Use more space between sentences than between words. Be careful to space your writing so tall letters do not run into descenders. Allow enough space for punctuation marks.

Oh, look! Ed's new computer is here.

Oh, look! Ed's new computer is here.

Are you sure? Call to let him know.

Are you sure? Call to let him know.

Name _____

Review

The computer screen shows the names of the students in Ms. Olsen's class. Write their names in alphabetical order. Use cursive.

Name _____

Evaluation

Remember: Cursive capitals **A**, **C**, and **E** should be joined to the letters that follow them. Also, leave enough space between words in your sentences.

Write the sentences.

Computers make writing fun for Al.

Adjust the monitor.

Are Omar and Eva using computer C?

✓ **Check Your Handwriting**   Yes   No

Do your capitals **A**, **C**, and **E** join the letters that follow them?   ☐   ☐

Did you leave enough space between words in your sentences?   ☐   ☐

Name _____

Writing Cursive H and K

You can see manuscript **H** and **K** in cursive **H** and **K**.
Trace and write the letters.

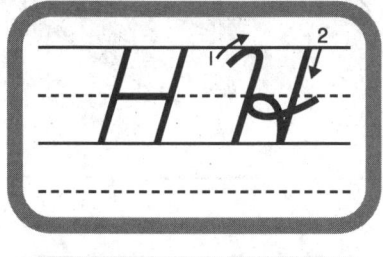 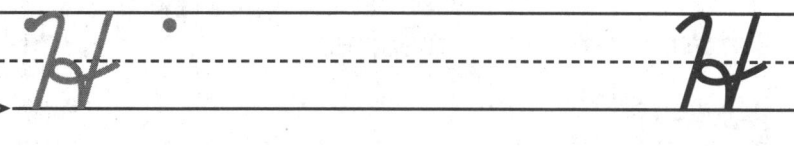

 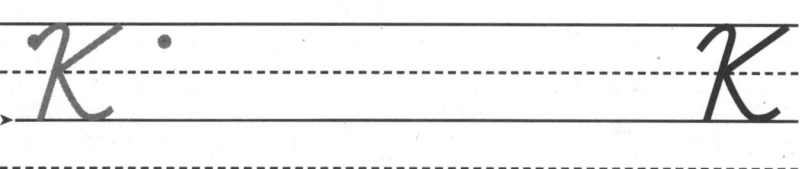

Trace and write the names of the cities and states.
Join **K** to the letter that follows it, but do not join **H**.

Halfway, Kentucky

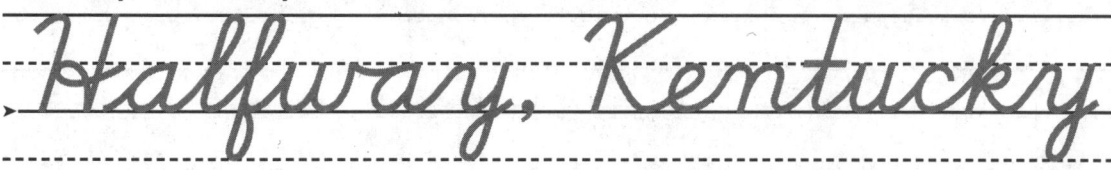

Kansas City, Kansas

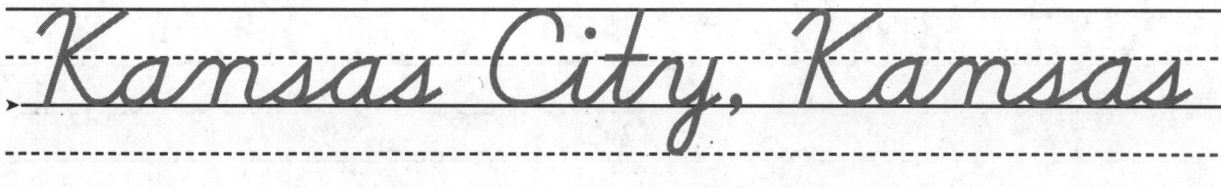

Letter Descriptions H: Start below the top; make a cane. Top start, to the right; down, up, left, touch, loop right, through, and stop. **K:** Start below the top; make a cane. Top start, to the right; slant down left, touch, slant down right, and up.

Name _____

Practicing Cursive H and K

Trace and write the sentences.

Kit visited Kentucky.

Kit visited Kentucky.

Historic sites were seen in Harrodsburg.

Historic sites were seen in Harrodsburg.

Horses were what Kit enjoyed most.

Horses were what Kit enjoyed most.

Name _____

Writing Cursive N, M, and U

Cursive **N** and **M** look a little like manuscript **N** and **M**. Cursive **U** looks very much like manuscript **U**. Trace and write the letters.

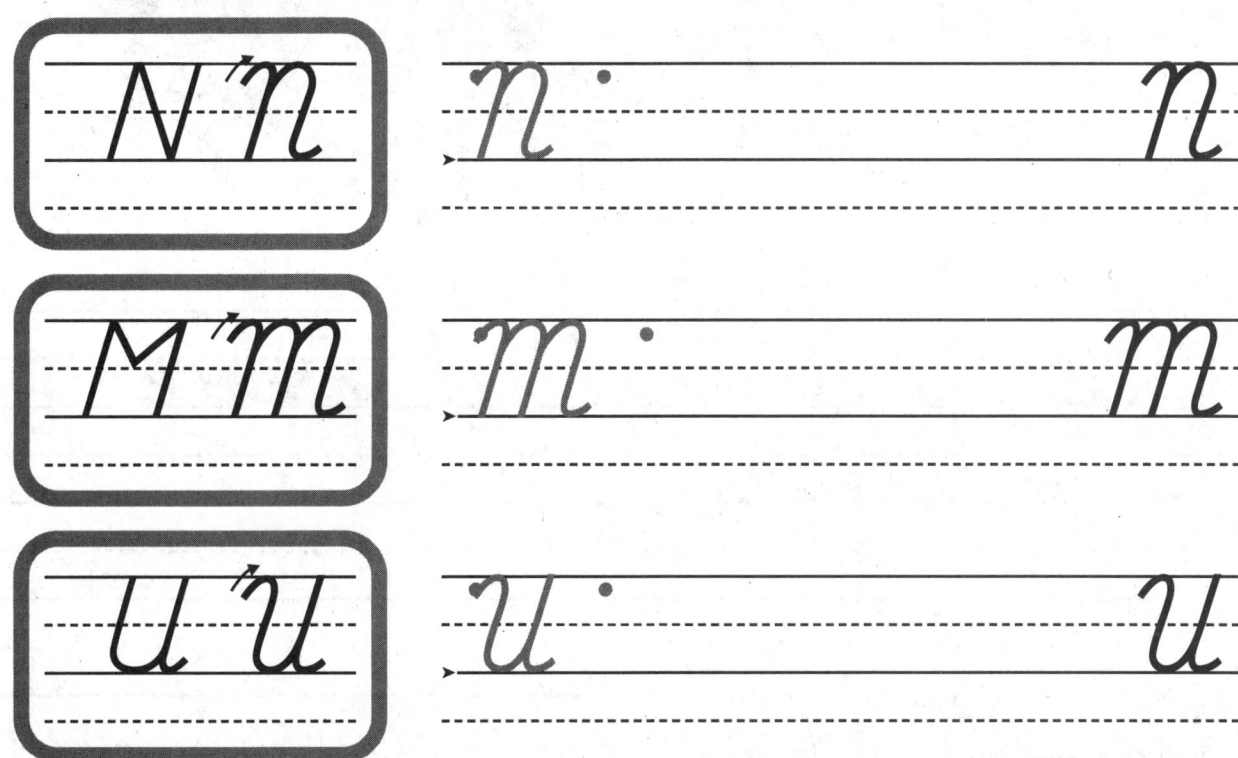

Trace and write the sentence. Always join **N, M,** and **U** to the letters that follow them.

New Mexico and Utah are states.

Letter Descriptions N: Start below the top; make a cane, up over the hill, and up. **M:** Start below the top; make a cane, up over the hill, up over the hill again, and up. **U:** Start below the top; make a cane, around, up, down, and up.

Name _____

Practicing Cursive N, M, and U

Trace and write the sentences.

Ned and Mia hike in Utah.

Ned and Mia hike in Utah.

Mia goes riding with Uncle Mark.

Mia goes riding with Uncle Mark.

Ned feeds a horse.

Ned feeds a horse.

Name _____

Writing Cursive V, W, and Y

Cursive **V, W,** and **Y** look a little like manuscript **V, W,** and **Y.** Trace and write the letters.

Trace and write the sentence. Remember to join cursive **Y** to the letter that follows it, but do not join **V** or **W.**

The Yakima Valley is in Washington.

Letter Descriptions V: Start below the top; make a cane, around, slant up right, sidestroke, and stop. **W:** Start below the top; make a cane, around, up, down, around, up again, sidestroke, and stop. **Y:** Start below the top; make a cane, around, up, down under water, loop up left, and through.

Name _____

Practicing Cursive V, W, and Y

Trace and write the sentences.

Val and Wendy go to national parks.

Val and Wendy go to national parks.

Wednesday they left for Yellowstone.

Wednesday they left for Yellowstone.

Yosemite is next.

Yosemite is next.

Name _____

Review

Mrs. Hart's class is making a list of places they would like to visit. Look at the names. Write them in the order you would choose to visit them.

| United Nations | Wildlife Kingdom | Hawaii |
| Yosemite | Museum of History | Mount Vernon |

1. _____
2. _____
3. _____
4. _____
5. _____
6. _____

Name _____

Evaluation

Write the sentences.

Remember: Cursive capital letters **H, V,** and **W** do not join the letters that follow. Also, all capital letters should touch the top and bottom lines.

Mel views Vermont.

Will likes Kentucky's beautiful horses.

Holly and Vic hike near Utica, New York.

✓ **Check Your Handwriting**   Yes   No

   Did you remember not to join capital letters
   H, V, and **W** to the letters that follow?   ☐   ☐

   Do all of your capital letters touch the top
   and bottom lines?   ☐   ☐

Name _____

Writing Cursive T and F

Cursive **T** and **F** look a little like manuscript **T** and **F**.
Trace and write the letters.

Trace and write the proper nouns. **T** and **F** are not joined to the letters that follow them.

Tina Ford

Tina Ford

Fort Worth, Texas

Fort Worth, Texas

Tallahassee, Florida

Tallahassee, Florida

Letter Descriptions T: Start below the top; down, around, up, and sidestroke. Wavy cross. **F:** Start below the top; down, around, up, and sidestroke. Wavy cross and a straight cross.

Name _____

Practicing Cursive T and F

Trace and write the sentences.

The Topps started to recycle in February.

The Topps started to recycle in February.

Trash day is Friday.

Trash day is Friday.

Tuesday is Toledo's day for glass pickup.

Tuesday is Toledo's day for glass pickup.

82

Name _____

Writing Cursive B, P, and R

Cursive **B**, **P**, and **R** look like manuscript **B**, **P**, and **R**.
Trace and write the letters.

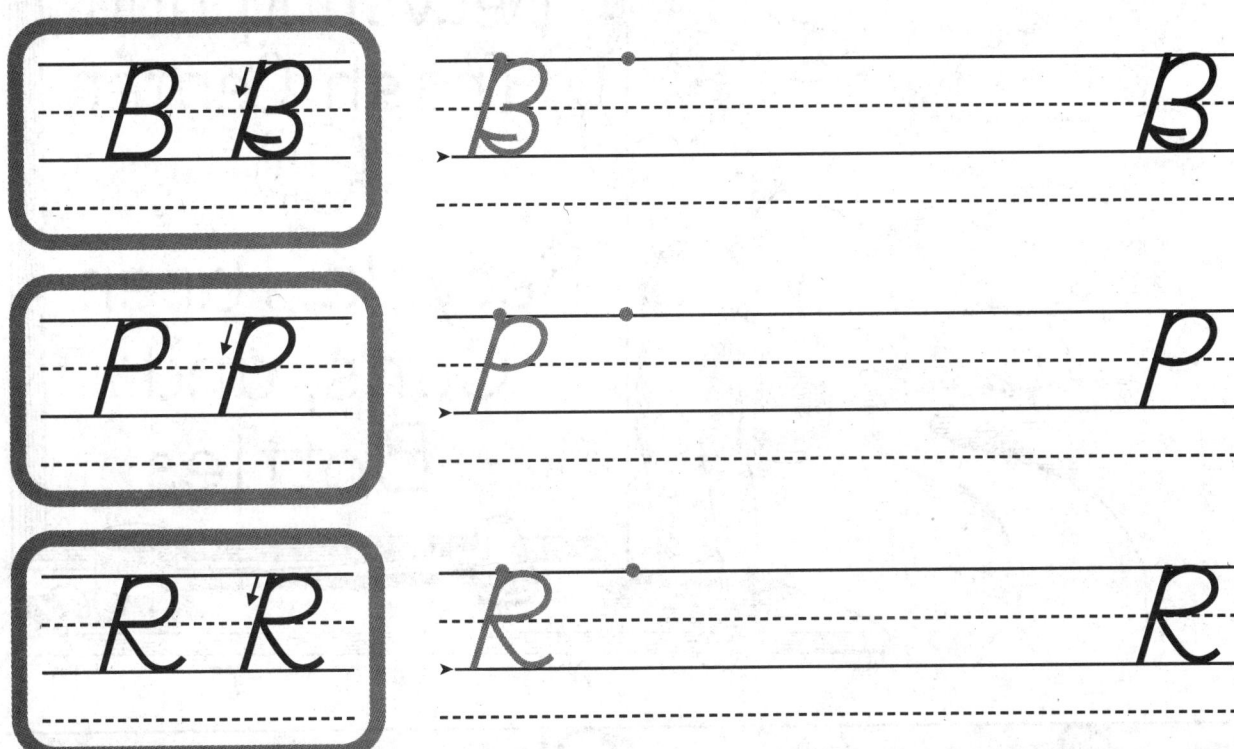

Trace and write the names. Do not join **B** and **P** to the letters that follow them. Always join **R** to the letter that follows it.

Rita Booth

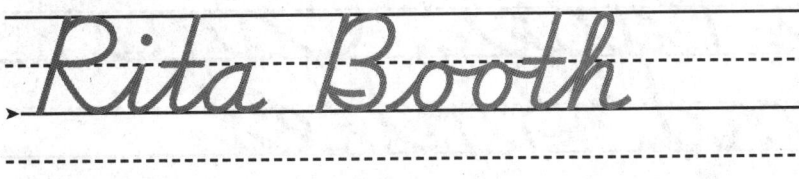

Brian

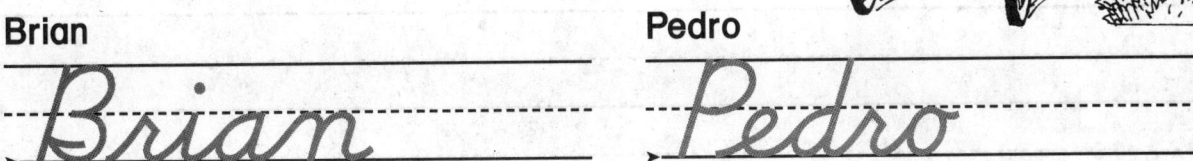

Pedro

Letter Descriptions B: Top start; down, up, around halfway, around again, touch, sidestroke, and stop.
P: Top start; down, up, around halfway, and close. **R:** Top start; down, up, around halfway, close, slant down right, and up.

Name _____

Practicing Cursive B, P, and R

Trace and write the words in the sign.

Brown's
Recycling and
Trash Center
Recycle Paper,
Cans, and
Bottles

Brown's Recycling and Trash Center Recycle Paper, Cans, and Bottles

84

Name _____

Review

Write what the person says next to each picture.

"Plant a tree," says Terry.
"Turn off the water," reminds Flo.
"Recycle newspapers," says Bonita.

Name _____

Evaluation

Remember: Do not join **T, F, B,** and **P** to the letters that follow. Also, leave enough space between sentences.

Write this news to send in to the newspaper:

The children on Pear Road surprised their neighbors this week. For one hour they offered free recycling bags. Boys and girls agreed: Free bags help the program.

✓ **Check Your Handwriting**   Yes   No

Did you remember not to connect **T, F, B,** and **P** to the letters that follow?   ☐   ☐

Did you leave enough space between sentences?   ☐   ☐

86

Name _____

Writing Cursive G, S, and I

Cursive **G**, **S**, and **I** do not look like manuscript **G**, **S**, and **I**. Trace and write the letters.

Trace and write the names. Do not join **G** and **S** to the letters that follow them. Always join **I** to the letter that follows it. Remember that the pronoun **I** is always capitalized.

Sir Isaac Newton
Galilei Galileo

Letter Descriptions G: Bottom start; uphill high, loop through the middle, up, curve down, around, through the uphill, sidestroke, and stop. **S:** Bottom start; uphill high, loop through the middle, curve down, around, through the uphill, sidestroke, and stop. **I:** Start below the middle; sidestroke left, curve down, around, uphill high, loop down, and up.

Name _____

Practicing Cursive G, S, and I

Trace and write the sentences.

Saturn

Gil drew a planet.

Gil drew a planet.

Sara and I studied Saturn's rings.

Sara and I studied Saturn's rings.

Spaceships interested Gina and Ivan.

Spaceships interested Gina and Ivan.

Name _____

Writing Cursive Q, Z, and D

Cursive **Q** and **Z** do not look like manuscript **Q** and **Z**. Cursive **D** looks something like manuscript **D**. Trace and write the letters.

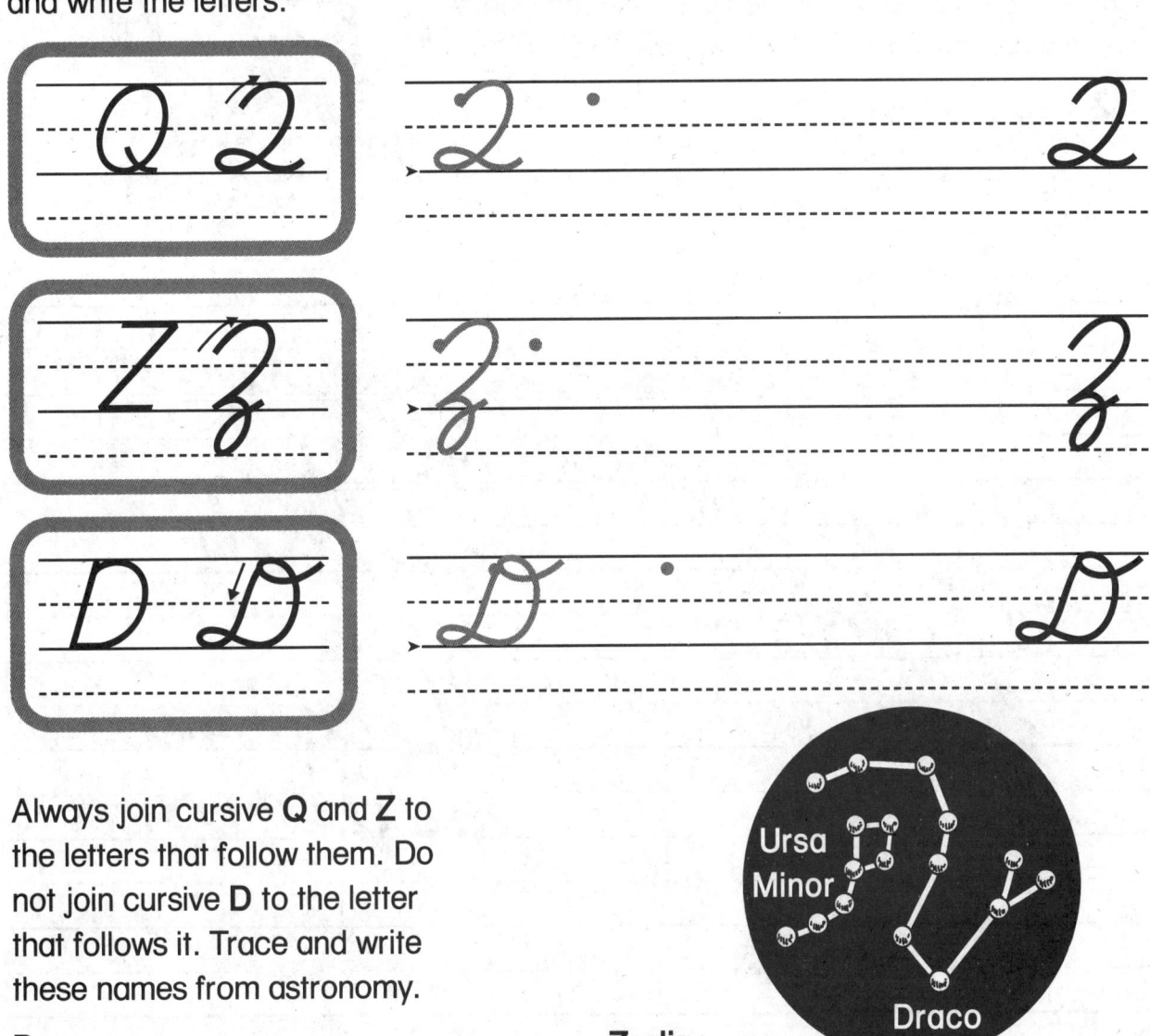

Always join cursive **Q** and **Z** to the letters that follow them. Do not join cursive **D** to the letter that follows it. Trace and write these names from astronomy.

Draco

Zodiac

Letter Descriptions Q: Start below the top; curve up, around, down, loop right, and up. Z: Start below the top; curve up, around, down, around again, and down under water, loop up left, and through. D: Top start; down, loop right, curve up, around, close, loop right, through, and stop.

89

Name _____

Practicing Cursive Q, Z, and D

Several students in Mr. Dennison's class worked on a report titled *The Space Shuttle Discovery*. They all signed their names under the title. Trace and write the title and the names. Underline the title.

The Space Shuttle Discovery
Zack   Quan
Debbie   Zoe
Zelda   Diana
Dick   Quinn

The Space Shuttle Discovery
Zack   Quan
Debbie   Zoe
Zelda   Diana
Dick   Quinn

Name _____

Writing Cursive J, X, and L

Cursive **J** does not look like manuscript **J**. You can see cursive **X** in manuscript **X**. Cursive **L** looks something like manuscript **L**. Trace and write the letters.

Trace and write the sentence. Always join **J** and **L** to the letters that follow them. Do not join **X** to the letter that follows it.

Jim Lovell was a Gemini astronaut.

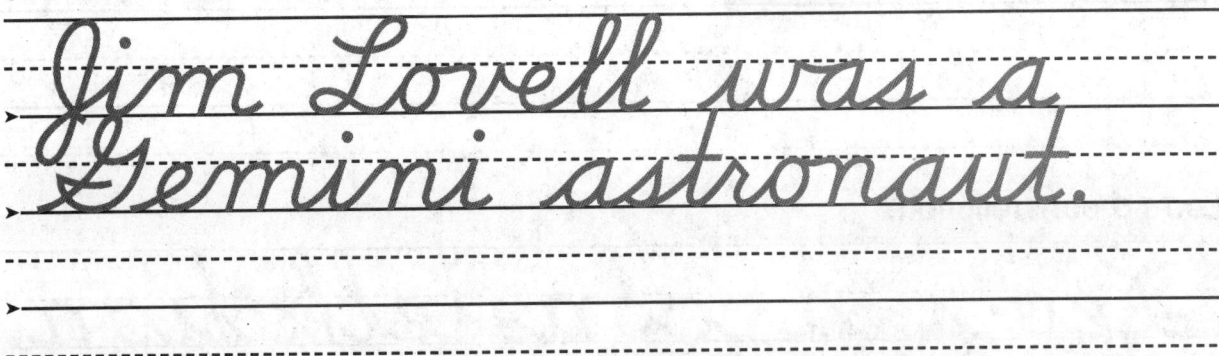

Letter Descriptions J: Bottom start; curve up, around, touch on the way down under water, loop up left, and through. **X:** Start below the top; curve up, slant down right, and up. Cross down left. **L:** Start below the top; uphill, loop down, loop right, and up.

91

Name _____

Practicing Cursive J, X, and L

Trace and write the sentences.

Scientists study X rays from stars.

Scientists study X rays from stars.

Jupiter is the largest planet.

Jupiter is the largest planet.

Leo's a constellation.

Leo's a constellation.

Name _____

Review

The children in Mr. Clemson's class wanted to have outer-space nicknames. Match children with nicknames that begin with the same letter. The first one is done for you.

Names		Nicknames	
Dina	Sue	Gemini	Scorpio
Leona	Gabe	Icarus	Quasar
Ira	Zubin	Zodiac	Dog Star
Jeri	Quin	Jupiter	Libra

Dina   *Dog Star*

Make up and write a nickname for Xavier to use.

Name _____

Evaluation

Remember: Make your letters the right size. Slant all your letters and punctuation marks in the same direction.

Write the sentences.

Quinn, Zoe, and I put an X on Mars.

Are Lars and Gina studying Saturn?

One of Jupiter's moons is Io.

✓ **Check Your Handwriting**   Yes   No
  Did you make your letters the right size? ☐ ☐
  Do your letters and punctuation marks
  slant the same way? ☐ ☐

Index

Alphabetical order, 71
Capitalization
  names, *(See proper nouns.)*
  pronoun *I,* 23, 87
  titles
    books, 15, 18
    people, 23, 87
    report, 90
Critical thinking, 14, 18, 20, 28, 29, 43, 51, 61, 79, 85, 93
Cross-curricular connections
  computers, 64–72
  health, 45, 46, 50, 52
  music, 40, 53–62
  science, 68, 69, 72, 82, 84–89, 91–94
  social studies, 16, 20, 24, 28, 40, 65, 67, 73–81
Descenders, 12, 35, 52, 63, 70
Evaluation of handwriting, 7, 30, 44, 52, 62, 72, 80, 86, 94
Legibility
  letter and word spacing, 7, 14, 36, 44, 69, 72, 86
  letter size and form, 7, 12, 35, 44, 52, 62, 63, 80, 94
  letter slant, 7, 13, 30, 36, 64, 94
  sentence spacing, 70, 86
Letter and word spacing, 7, 14, 36, 44, 69, 72, 86
Letter descriptions, 8–11
Letter size and form, 7, 12, 35, 44, 52, 62, 63, 80, 94
Letter slant, 7, 13, 30, 36, 64, 94
Letters
  cursive capitals
    A, 65–66; **B,** 83–84;
    C, 65–66; **D,** 89–90;
    E, 67–68; **F,** 81–82;
    G, 87–88; **H,** 73–74;
    I, 87–88; **J,** 91–92;
    K, 73–74; **L,** 91–92;
    M, 75–76; **N,** 75–76;
    O, 67–68; **P,** 83–84;
    Q, 89–90; **R,** 83–84;
    S, 87–88; **T,** 81–82;
    U, 75–76; **V,** 77–78;
    W, 77–78; **X,** 91–92;
    Y, 77–78; **Z,** 89–90

  cursive lower-case
    a, 45–46; **b,** 53–54;
    c, 45–46; **d,** 45–46;
    e, 39–40; **f,** 59–60;
    g, 49–50; **h,** 37–38;
    i, 39–40; **j,** 41–42;
    k, 37–38; **l,** 37–38;
    m, 47–48; **n,** 47–48;
    o, 53–54; **p,** 41–42;
    q, 49–50; **r,** 57–58;
    s, 57–58; **t,** 37–38;
    u, 39–40; **v,** 55–56;
    w, 53–54; **x,** 47–48;
    y, 49–50; **z,** 55–56

  manuscript
    aA, 15–16; **bB,** 19–20;
    cC, 17–18; **dD,** 15–16;
    eE, 17–18; **fF,** 19–20;
    gG, 15–16; **hH,** 21–22;
    iI, 23–24; **jJ,** 25–26;
    kK, 21–22; **lL,** 19–20;
    mM, 25–26; **nN,** 25–26;
    oO, 15–16; **pP,** 25–26;
    qQ, 27–28; **rR,** 25–26;
    sS, 17–18; **tT,** 21–22;
    uU, 23–24; **vV,** 27–28;
    wW, 23–24; **xX,** 27–28;
    yY, 23–24; **zZ,** 27–28
Number descriptions, 9
Proper nouns, 16, 17, 19, 20, 21, 22, 23, 24, 26, 27, 28, 29, 30, 31, 65, 66, 67, 68, 70, 71, 72, 73, 74, 75, 76, 77, 78, 79, 80, 81, 82, 83, 84, 85, 86, 87, 88, 89, 90, 91, 92, 93, 94
Punctuation practice
  apostrophe, 14, 19, 20, 28, 58, 66, 70, 80, 82, 84, 88, 92, 94
  colon, 64, 86
  comma, 65, 67, 70, 73, 80, 81, 84, 85, 94
  dollars and cents, 30
  exclamation mark, 14, 70
  hyphen, 30, 69
  period, 14, 20, 21, 23, 25, 26, 27, 30, 66, 68, 70, 72, 74, 75, 76, 77, 78, 80, 82, 85, 86, 88, 91, 92, 94

  question mark, 64, 70, 72, 94
  quotation marks, 20, 85
Review of handwriting, 29, 43, 51, 61, 71, 79, 85, 93
Sentence spacing, 70, 86
Strokes that make cursive letters
  ending, 32, 33, 41, 49
  joining, 31, 32, 33, 34, 38, 53, 62, 67, 72, 73, 75, 77, 80, 81, 83, 86, 87, 89, 91
  overhill, 5, 33, 34, 45, 47, 49, 53
  sidestroke, 5, 34, 53, 55
  uphill, 5, 32, 33, 34, 37, 39, 41, 53
Themes
  cities and states, 73–80, 81, 82
  computers, 64–72
  dogs, 12, 14–30
  Hawaii, 37–38, 40–41, 43–44
  music, 53–62
  outdoor activities, 45–52
  outer space, 87–94
  recycling, 81–86
Transition to cursive, 5, 31–36
Workbook features, 6
Writing, functional/everyday
  alphabetical order, 71
  billboard, 84
  captions, 85
  classifying, 51
  directions, 43
  letter, 24
  lists, 20, 29, 51, 61, 79
  lost-dog notice, 22
  matching names and actions, 26
  newspaper notice, 86
  store names, 28
  titles of books, 15, 18
Writing posture, 4